Planning for Learning in Early Years

A Practical Approach to Development Matters

Nicky Simmons & Ginny Morris

First Edition: March 2016

© 2016 Nicky Simmons & Ginny Morris
All rights reserved.

ISBN: 1530228010
ISBN-13:   978-1530228010

About The Authors

Ginny Morris

Ginny has a wide range of experience teaching Early Years in both mainstream and special school settings. She was the leader of a highly successful Foundation Unit for seven years, during which time she also supported & mentored other Early Years settings within the Local Authority.

Nicky Simmons

Nicky was a Primary School Head Teacher for ten years. During her headship she provided a strategic vision for the school, transforming it into a dynamic learning environment. She was renown for her charismatic style and solution focused approach.

Nicky & Ginny now run their own company, Morris & Simmons Education. They write & deliver a wide program of professional development workshops & produce their own creative resources for Early Years practitioners. As well as organising their own open workshops, they are also regularly invited to work in different settings on Improvement Projects. They offer simple solutions, model good practice and coach practitioners to help them improve their provision.

Nicky & Ginny are delighted that they are able to share their knowledge, experience and expertise with a wider audience through, what they hope to be, one of many publications. For more information about their work visit their website www.morrissimmons.com or email mse@morrissimmons.com

Acknowledgements

Throughout our careers we have been privileged to work with so many talented colleagues, children and families, many of whom have significantly contributed to our expertise. We are very grateful for their challenge, inspiration and belief in our abilities, always pushing us to reach new heights.

We would particularly like to acknowledge those settings who took the time to provide us with very valuable feedback on this publication: Arley Primary School, Holbrook Primary School, St Paul's C of E Primary School, The Cannons C of E Primary School, Kineton C of E Primary School and Provost Williams C of E Primary School.

Finally we would like to thank our families without whose support, encouragement and technical expertise none of this work would have been possible.

How To Use This Book

This book was written to help all practitioners working with young children recognise and clearly identify the learning steps within and across each band of Development Matters. Vital steps are too often often missed in children's development and as a result gaps in learning appear. Taking each Development Matters descriptor we have translated them into simple *"I am learning to"* statements that are easy to use in every day planning.

When you are planning activities for young children, the ability to generate an appropriate and specific learning statement is essential to provide the hook for practitioners to :

- Engage in deeper level learning with children by posing relevant and challenging questions
- Identify and resolve misconceptions
- Pin point next steps in learning
- Measure progress

Laid out in 3 distinct columns simple learning statements are matched to Development Matters descriptors with a 'Looking Ahead' column to help the practitioner visualise where children are heading. The purple highlighted statements in the Development Matters do not have a Learning Statement related to them as they are behaviours that you would observe children demonstrating, as they develop and mature over time.

Although the Learning Statements have been designed to match Development Matters descriptors they do not have to be followed in the sequence in which they are written and the Learning Statements are not time limited or context specific. Activities will often change but the learning may well need to remain the same.

Planning for Learning in Early Years

Contents

Characteristics of Effective Learning — page 1

Personal, Social & Emotional Development — page 7

Communication & Language — page 21

Physical Development — page 35

Literacy — page 45

Mathematics — page 55

Understanding the World — page 65

Expressive Arts & Design — page 79

Planning for Learning in Early Years

Characteristics of Effective Learning

Planning for Learning - Characteristics of Effective Learning - Playing & Exploring

Development Matters: Unique Child	Suggested Learning Statements
Playing and Exploring: *Engagement*	
Finding out and exploring * Showing curiosity about objects, events and people * Using senses to explore the world around them * Engaging in open-ended activity * Showing particular interests	I am learning to explore I am learning to investigate I am learning to find out more about something I am learning to use resources in unique and interesting ways I am learning to combine resources in my play I am learning to communicate my interests I am learning to pretend that objects are something else I am learning to act out my experiences with others I am learning to use my experiences in my play I am learning to try new things I am learning to take risks I am learning about making mistakes I am learning to tackle things that may be difficult I am learning that when I practise things I can get better
Playing with what they know * Pretending objects are things from their experience * Representing their experiences in play * Taking on a role in their play * Acting out experiences with other people	
Being willing to 'have a go' * Initiating activities * Seeking challenge * Showing a 'can do' attitude * Taking a risk, engaging in new experiences, and learning by trial and error	

Planning for Learning - Characteristics of Effective Learning

Development Matters: Observing how a child is learning	Suggested Learning Statements
Active Learning: *Motivation*	

Being involved and concentrating ✳ Maintaining focus on their activity for a period of time ✳ Showing high levels of energy, fascination ✳ Not easily distracted ✳ Paying attention to details	I am learning to concentrate I am learning to ignore distractions I am learning to notice things in more detail I am learning to choose the things that really fascinate me I am learning to persist even when things get difficult I am learning to try different ways of doing things when one approach doesn't work I am learning to be resilient when things get difficult I am learning to talk about how I feel when I have overcome a challenge I am learning to talk about when I feel proud
Keeping on trying ✳ Persisting with activity when challenges occur ✳ Showing a belief that more effort or a different approach with pay off ✳ Bouncing back after difficulties	
Enjoying achieving what they set out to do ✳ Showing satisfaction in meeting their own goals ✳ Being proud of how they accomplished something - not just the end result ✳ Enjoying meeting challenges for their own sake rather than external rewards or praise	

Planning for Learning - Characteristics of Effective Learning - Creating & Thinking Critically

Development Matters: Unique Child	Suggested Learning Statements
Creating and Thinking Critically: *Thinking*	
Having their own ideas * Thinking of ideas * Finding ways to solve problems * Finding new ways to do things	I am learning to think of my own ideas I am learning to talk about the problems I encounter and find ways to solve them I am learning to find different ways to do things I am learning to talk about my thinking
Making Links * Making links and noticing patterns in their experience * Making predictions * Testing their ideas * Developing ideas of grouping, sequences, cause and effect	I am learning to talk about how and what I am learning I am learning to predict I am learning to set hypotheses and test out my ideas I am learning to recognise when my previous learning or experiences link to what I am doing
Choosing ways to do things * Planning, making decisions about how to approach a task, solve a problem and reach a goal * Checking how well their activities are going * Changing strategy as needed * Reviewing how well the approach worked	I am learning to plan I am learning to make decisions I am learning to reflect on how I have tackled a task and how well it is going I am learning to change my strategy where necessary

Personal, Social & Emotional Development

Planning for Learning - Personal, Social & Emotional Development: Making Relationships

Development Matters: Unique Child	Suggested Learning Statements	Looking Ahead
Birth - 11 months * **Enjoys the company of others and seeks contact with others from birth** * Gazes at faces and copies facial movements e.g. sticking out tongue, opening mouth and widening eyes * Responds when talked to, e.g. moves arms and legs, changes facial expression, moves body and makes mouth movements * **Recognises and is most responsive to main carer's voice: face brightens, activity increases when familiar carer appears** * Responds to what carer is paying attention to e.g. following their gaze * **Likes cuddles and being held: calms, snuggles in, smiles, gazes at carer's face or strokes carer's skin** **8 - 20 months** * Seeks to gain attention in a variety of ways, drawing others into social interaction * **Builds relationships with special people** * **Is wary of unfamiliar people** * Interacts with others and explores new situations when supported by familiar person * **Shows interest in the activities of others and responds differently to children and adults e.g. may be more interested in watching children than adults or may pay more attention when children talk to them** **16 - 26 months** * Plays alongside others * Uses familiar adult as a secure base from which to explore independently in new environments e.g. ventures away to play and interact with others, but returns for a cuddle or reassurance if becomes anxious * Plays co-operatively with a familiar adult e.g. rolling a ball back and forth	I am learning to copy facial movements I am learning to respond when someone talks to me I am learning to respond to what an adult is paying attention to I am learning to gain attention from others I am learning to interact with adults and other children I am learning to explore new situations I am learning to play alongside others I am learning to explore my environment without adult support for short periods of time I am learning to take turns with an adult in my play	**22 - 36 months** * Interested in others' play and starting to join in * **Seeks out others to share experiences** * **Shows affection and concern for people who are special to them** * **May form a special friendship with another child** **30 - 50 months** * Can play in a group, extending and elaborating play ideas e.g. building up a role-play activity with other children * Initiates play offering cues to peers to join them * Keeps play going by responding to what others are saying or doing * **Demonstrates friendly behaviour, initiating conversations and forming good relationships with peers and familiar adults**

Planning for Learning - Personal, Social & Emotional Development: Making Relationships

Development Matters: Unique Child	Suggested Learning Statements	Looking Ahead
22 - 36 months ✳ Interested in others' play and starting to join in ✳ **Seeks out others to share experiences** ✳ **Shows affection and concern for people who are special to them** ✳ **May form a special friendship with another child**	I am learning to join in with others during my play I am learning to make choices about who I play with	**EYFS - ELG** ✳ Children play co-operatively , taking turns with others ✳ They take account of one another's ideas about how to organise their activity ✳ They show sensitivity to others' needs and feelings, and form positive relationships with adults and other children **EYFS - EXCEEDING** ★ Children play group games with rules. ★ They understand someone else's point of view can be different from theirs. ★ They resolve minor disagreements through listening to each other to come up with a fair solution. ★ They understand what bullying is and that this is unacceptable behaviour.
30 - 50 months ✳ Can play in a group, extending and elaborating play ideas e.g. building up a role-play activity with other children ✳ Initiates play offering cues to peers to join them ✳ Keeps play going by responding to what others are saying or doing ✳ **Demonstrates friendly behaviour, initiating conversations and forming good relationships with peers and familiar adults**	I am learning to play in a group I am learning to extend a play idea I am learning to think of my own ideas in my play I am learning to invite other children to play with me I am learning to talk to others in my play	

Planning for Learning in Early Years

Planning for Learning - Personal, Social & Emotional Development: Making Relationships

Development Matters: Unique Child	Suggested Learning Statements	Looking Ahead
40 - 60 months ✽ Initiates conversation, attends to and takes account of what others say ✽ Explains own knowledge and understanding and asks appropriate questions of others ✽ Takes steps to resolve conflicts with other children e.g. finding a compromise **EYFS - ELG** ✽ Children play co-operatively, taking turns with others ✽ They take account of one another's ideas about how to organise their activity ✽ They show sensitivity to others' needs and feelings, and form positive relationships with adults and other children	I am learning to start a conversation and listen to what others say I am learning to explain what I know and understand I am learning to ask questions I am learning to listen to others and find ways to resolve conflicts I am learning to play co-operatively I am learning to take turns I am learning to listen to other people's ideas and include them in my play I am learning to think about how other people feel when making decisions and choices I am learning to follow rules when playing games I am learning that other people might think differently to me I am learning to sort out problems by listening to others I am learning to understand what bullying is I am learning that bullying is wrong	**EYFS - EXCEEDING** ★ Children play group games with rules. ★ They understand someone else's point of view can be different from theirs. ★ They resolve minor disagreements through listening to each other to come up with a fair solution. ★ They understand what bullying is and that this is unacceptable behaviour.

Planning for Learning - Personal, Social & Emotional Development: Self-confidence & self-awareness

Development Matters: Unique Child	Suggested Learning Statements	Looking Ahead
Birth - 11 months * **Laughs and gurgles e.g. shows pleasure at being tickled and other physical interactions** * Uses voice, gesture, eye contact and facial expression to make contact with people and keep their attention	I am learning to use my voice, gesture and facial expression to gain and keep other people's attention	**22 - 36 months** * Separates from main carer with support and encouragement from a familiar adult * Expresses own preferences and interests
8 - 20 months * Enjoys finding own nose, eyes or tummy as part of naming games * Learns that own voice and actions have effects on others * Uses pointing with eye gaze to make requests, and to share an interest * Engages other person to help achieve a goal, e.g. to get an object out of reach	I am learning to locate my own body parts I am learning to use my voice and actions to have an effect on others I am learning to point and eye gaze to communicate I am learning to get someone's attention to help me achieve a goal	**30 - 50 months** * Can select and use activities and resources with help * **Welcomes and values praise for what they have done** * Enjoys responsibility of carrying out small tasks * Is more outgoing towards unfamiliar people and more confident in new social situations * Confident to talk to other children when playing and will communicate freely about own home and community * Shows confidence in asking adults for help
16 - 26 months * **Explores new toys and environments, but 'checks in' regularly with familiar adult as and when needed** * Gradually able to engage in pretend play with toys (supports child to understand their own thinking may be different from others) * **Demonstrates sense of self as an individual e.g. wants to do things independently, says 'No' to adult**	I am learning to play simple pretend games with support	

Planning for Learning - Personal, Social & Emotional Development: Self-confidence & self-awareness

Development Matters: Unique Child	Suggested Learning Statements	Looking Ahead
22 - 36 months ∗ Separates from main carer with support and encouragement from a familiar adult ∗ Expresses own preferences and interests	I am learning to separate from my main carer I am learning to show others what I like and what interests me	**EYFS - ELG** ∗ Children are confident to try new activities, and say why they like some activities more than others ∗ They are confident to speak in a familiar group, will talk about their ideas, and will choose the resources they need for their chosen activities ∗ They say when they do or don't need help
30 - 50 months ∗ Can select and use activities and resources with help ∗ **Welcomes and values praise for what they have done** ∗ Enjoys responsibility of carrying out small tasks ∗ Is more outgoing towards unfamiliar people and more confident in new social situations ∗ Confident to talk to other children when playing and will communicate freely about own home and community ∗ Shows confidence in asking adults for help	I am learning to choose activities and resources with help I am learning to carry out tasks for others I am learning to talk to people who I don't know very well I am learning to talk to children that I am playing with I am learning to talk about myself and my home I am learning to ask for help when I need it	**EYFS - EXCEEDING** ★ Children are confident to speak to a class group. They can talk about things they enjoy and are good at, and about things they do not find easy ★ They are resourceful in finding support when they need help or information ★ They can talk about the plans they have made to carry out activities and what they might change if they were to repeat them

Planning for Learning - Personal, Social & Emotional Development: Self-confidence & self-awareness

Development Matters: Unique Child	Suggested Learning Statements	Looking Ahead
40 - 60 months ∗ Confident to speak to others about own needs, wants, interests and opinions ∗ Can describe self in positive terms and talk about abilities **EYFS - ELG** ∗ Children are confident to try new activities, and say why they like some activities more than others ∗ They are confident to speak in a familiar group, will talk about their ideas, and will choose the resources they need for their chosen activities ∗ They say when they do or don't need help	I am learning to talk to other people about what I need and want I am learning to talk to other people about what I am interested in and what I think I am learning to talk about what I am good at I am learning to try new activities and say why I like some of them I am learning to talk about my ideas I am learning to choose the resources I need I am learning to decide for myself when I do and do not need help I am learning to talk in front of others I am learning to speak confidently in front of others I am learning to talk about what I'm good at and what I find more difficult I am learning to be resourceful I am learning to talk about the plans I have made and any improvements I could make	**EYFS - EXCEEDING** ★ Children are confident to speak to a class group. They can talk about things they enjoy and are good at, and about things they do not find easy ★ They are resourceful in finding support when they need help or information ★ They can talk about the plans they have made to carry out activities and what they might change if they were to repeat them

Planning for Learning - Personal, Social & Emotional Development: Managing Feelings & Behaviour

Development Matters: Unique Child	Suggested Learning Statements	Looking Ahead
Birth - 11 months * **Is comforted by touch and people's faces and voices** * **Seeks physical and emotional comfort by snuggling into trusted adults** * **Calms from being upset when held, rocked, spoken or sung to with soothing voice** * **Shows a range of emotions such as pleasure, fear and excitement** * **Reacts emotionally to other people's emotions e.g. smiles when smiled at and becomes distressed if hears another child crying** **8 - 20 months** * **Uses familiar adult to share feelings such as excitement or pleasure, and for 'emotional refuelling' when feeling tired, stressed or frustrated** * Growing ability to sooth themselves and may like to use a comfort object * Co-operates with caregiving experiences e.g. dressing * Beginning to understand 'yes', 'no' and some boundaries **16 - 26 months** * Is aware of others' feelings, e.g. looks concerned if hears crying or looks excited if hears a familiar happy voice * **Growing sense of will and determination may result in feelings of anger and frustration which are difficult to handle e.g. may have tantrums** * Responds to a few appropriate boundaries with encouragement and support * Begins to learn that some things are theirs, some things are shared and some things belong to other people	I am learning to soothe myself after being distressed I am learning to co-operate when being dressed or changed I am learning to understand some things that I am and am not allowed to do I am learning to respond to the words 'yes' & 'no' I am learning to notice others' emotions I am learning to respond to some simple boundaries and rules with support I am learning to recognise that not everything is 'mine'	**22 - 36 months** * **Seeks comfort from familiar adults when needed** * Can express their own feelings such as sad, happy, cross, scared, worried * Responds to the feelings and wishes of others * Aware that some actions can hurt or harm others * Tries to help or give comfort when others are distressed * Shows understanding and co-operates with some boundaries and routines * Can inhibit own actions/behaviours e.g. stop themselves from doing something they shouldn't do * Growing ability to distract self when upset e.g. by engaging in a new play activity **30 - 50 months** * Aware of own feelings, and knows that some actions and words can hurt others' feelings * Begins to accept the needs of others and can take turns and share resources, sometimes with support from others * Can usually tolerate delay when needs are not immediately met and understands wishes may not always be met * Can usually adapt behaviour to different events, social situations and changes in routine

Planning for Learning - Personal, Social & Emotional Development: Managing Feelings & Behaviour

Development Matters: Unique Child	Suggested Learning Statements	Looking Ahead
22 - 36 months ✳ **Seeks comfort from familiar adults when needed** ✳ Can express their own feelings such as sad, happy, cross, scared, worried ✳ Responds to the feelings and wishes of others ✳ Aware that some actions can hurt or harm others ✳ Tries to help or give comfort when others are distressed ✳ Shows understanding and co-operates with some boundaries and routines ✳ Can inhibit own actions/behaviours e.g. stop themselves from doing something they shouldn't do ✳ Growing ability to distract self when upset e.g. by engaging in a new play activity	I am learning to show how I feel I am learning to respond to the wishes and feelings of others I am learning to follow some rules and routines I am learning to stop when I am doing something I shouldn't I am learning to distract myself when I'm upset	**EYFS - ELG** ✳ Children talk about how they and others show feelings, talk about their own and others' behaviour and its consequences and know that some behaviour is unacceptable ✳ They work as part of a group or class and understand and follow the rules ✳ They adjust their behaviour to different situations and take changes of routine in their stride **EYFS - EXCEEDING** ★ Children know some ways to manage their feelings and are beginning to use these to maintain control ★ They can listen to each others' suggestions and plan how to achieve an outcome without adult help ★ They know when and how to stand up for themselves appropriately ★ They can stop and think before acting and they can wait for things they want
30 - 50 months ✳ Aware of own feelings, and knows that some actions and words can hurt others' feelings ✳ Begins to accept the needs of others and can take turns and share resources, sometimes with support from others ✳ Can usually tolerate delay when needs are not immediately met and understands wishes may not always be met ✳ Can usually adapt behaviour to different events, social situations and changes in routine	I am learning that my actions and words can affect others I am learning that I have different feelings I am learning to take turns and share with support I am learning to wait for my needs to be met I am learning that I need to behave differently in different situations	

Planning for Learning in Early Years

Planning for Learning - Personal, Social & Emotional Development: Managing Feelings & Behaviour

Development Matters: Unique Child	Suggested Learning Statements	Looking Ahead
40 - 60 months * Understands that own actions affect other people, e.g. becomes upset or tries to comfort another child when they realise they have upset them * Aware of the boundaries set, and of behavioural expectations in the setting * Beginning to be able to negotiate and solve problems without aggression e.g. when someone has taken their toy **EYFS - ELG** * Children talk about how they and others show feelings, talk about their own and others' behaviour and its consequences and know that some behaviour is unacceptable * They work as part of a group or class and understand and follow the rules * They adjust their behaviour to different situations and take changes of routine in their stride	I am learning that my actions can affect others I am learning that there are rules I am learning to talk to others to resolve a problem I am learning to talk about my own and others' feelings I am learning to talk about my own and others' behaviour and how this affects others I am learning the difference between good behaviour and that which is not I am learning to work as part of a group I am learning to follow the rules I am learning to change my behaviour to suit the situation I am learning to accept changes in routine I am learning to be more in control of my different emotions I am learning to listen to and take account of other people's suggestions independently I am learning to be more assertive I am learning to take time to think about what to do before I do it I am learning to be patient	**EYFS - EXCEEDING** ★ Children know some ways to manage their feelings and are beginning to use these to maintain control ★ They can listen to each others' suggestions and plan how to achieve an outcome without adult help ★ They know when and how to stand up for themselves appropriately ★ They can stop and think before acting and they can wait for things they want

Communication & Language

Planning for Learning - Communication & Language: Listening & Attention

Development Matters: Unique Child	Suggested Learning Statements	Looking Ahead
Birth - 11 months * Turns toward a familiar sound then locates a range of sounds with accuracy * Listens to, distinguishes and responds to intonations and sounds of voices * Reacts in interaction with others by smiling, looking and moving * Quietens or alerts to the sound of speech * Looks intently at a person talking, but stops responding if speaker turns away * Listens to familiar sounds, words or finger plays * **Fleeting Attention - not under child's control, new stimuli takes whole attention** **8 - 20 months** * Moves whole bodies to sounds they enjoy, such as music or a regular beat * **Has a strong exploratory impulse** * Concentrates intently on an object or activity of own choosing for short periods * **Pays attention to dominant stimulus - easily distracted by noises or other people talking** **16 - 26 months** * Listens to and enjoys rhythmic patterns in rhymes and stories * Enjoys rhymes and demonstrates listening by trying to join in with actions or vocalisations * **Rigid attention - may appear not to hear**	I am learning to turn my head in response to sound I am learning to locate sounds accurately I am learning to distinguish between different voices I am learning to respond to different voices I am learning to interact with others using non-verbal communication I am learning to respond to familiar sounds and words I am learning to respond to sounds that I enjoy I am learning to focus on something I choose for a short period of time I am learning to listen and respond to rhythmic patterns in rhymes and stories I am learning to join in with simple rhymes using actions and sounds	**22 - 36 months** * Listens with interest to the noises adults make when they read stories * Recognises and responds to many familiar sounds e.g. turning to a knock on the door, looking at or going to the door * **Shows interest in play with sounds, songs and rhymes** * **Single channelled attention. Can shift to a different task if attention fully obtained - using child's name helps focus** **30 - 50 months** * Listens to others one to one or in small groups, when conversation interests them * Listens to stories with increasing attention and recall * Joins in with repeated refrains and anticipates key events and phrases in rhymes and stories * **Focusing attention - still listen or do, but can shift own attention** * Is able to follow directions (if not intently focused on own choice of activity)

Planning for Learning - Communication & Language: Listening & Attention

Development Matters: Unique Child	Suggested Learning Statements	Looking Ahead
22 - 36 months ✴ Listens with interest to the noises adults make when they read stories ✴ Recognises and responds to many familiar sounds e.g. turning to a knock on the door, looking at or going to the door ✴ **Shows interest in play with sounds, songs and rhymes** ✴ **Single channelled attention. Can shift to a different task if attention fully obtained - using child's name helps focus**	I am learning to listen and respond to familiar sounds I am learning to respond to my name	**EYFS - ELG** ✴ Children can listen attentively in a range of situations ✴ They listen to stories accurately anticipating key events and respond to what they hear with relevant comments, questions or actions ✴ They give their attention to what others say and respond appropriately, while engaged in another activity
30 - 50 months ✴ Listens to others one to one or in small groups, when conversation interests them ✴ Listens to stories with increasing attention and recall ✴ Joins in with repeated refrains and anticipates key events and phrases in rhymes and stories ✴ **Focusing attention - still listen or do, but can shift own attention** ✴ Is able to follow directions (if not intently focused on own choice of activity)	I am learning to listen to simple conversation I am learning to listen carefully to a simple story I am learning to answer questions about a simple story I am learning to join in with a story or rhyme I am learning to follow simple instructions	**EYFS - EXCEEDING** ★ Children listen to instructions and follow them accurately, asking for clarification if necessary ★ They listen attentively with sustained concentration to follow a story without pictures or props and can listen in a larger group, for example, at assembly

Planning for Learning - Communication & Language: Listening & Attention

Development Matters: Unique Child	Suggested Learning Statements	Looking Ahead
40 - 60 months * Maintains attention, concentrates and sits quietly during appropriate activity * Two-channelled attention - can listen and do for short span **EYFS - ELG** * Children can listen attentively in a range of situations * They listen to stories accurately anticipating key events and respond to what they hear with relevant comments, questions or actions * They give their attention to what others say and respond appropriately, while engaged in another activity	I am learning to listen while I am doing something else I am learning to concentrate until an activity is completed I am learning to listen attentively I am learning to listen carefully to stories so that I can make sensible suggestions about what might happen I am learning to respond to stories that I have listened to by making comments I am learning to ask questions about the stories that I have listened to I am learning to listen carefully and respond appropriately when others are talking I am learning to listen and respond to more complex instructions I am learning to ask for help when I need it I am learning to listen for sustained periods of time without being distracted I am learning to listen attentively for a sustained period of time in a larger group I am learning to listen attentively to a story without any visual cues	**EYFS - EXCEEDING** ★ Children listen to instructions and follow them accurately, asking for clarification if necessary ★ They listen attentively with sustained concentration to follow a story without pictures or props and can listen in a larger group, for example, at assembly **Speaking & Listening Key Stage 1** (NOTE: these statements are used from Y1 - Y6) **Pupils should be taught to:** • Listen and respond appropriately to adults and their peers • Ask relevant questions to extend their understanding and build vocabulary and knowledge • Articulate and justify answers, arguments and opinions • Give well-structured descriptions and explanations • Maintain attention and participate actively in collaborative conversations, staying on topic and initiating and responding to comments • Use spoken language to develop understanding through speculating, hypothesising, imagining and exploring ideas • Speak audibly and fluently with an increasing command of Standard English • Participate in discussions, presentations, performances and debates • Gain, maintain and monitor the interest of the listener(s) • Consider and evaluate different viewpoints, attending to and building on the contribution of others • Select and use appropriate registers for effective communication

Planning for Learning - Communication & Language: Understanding

Development Matters: Unique Child	Suggested Learning Statements	Looking Ahead
Birth - 11 months * Stops and looks when hears own name * Starts to understand contextual clues e.g. familiar gestures, words and sounds **8 - 20 months** * Developing the ability to follow others' body language, including pointing and gesture * Responds to the different things said when in a familiar context with a special person (e.g. 'Where's mummy?' 'Where's your nose?') * Understanding of single words in context is developing e.g. 'cup', 'milk', 'daddy' **16 - 26 months** * Selects familiar objects by name and will go and find objects when asked, or identify objects from a group * Understands simple sentences (e.g. 'Throw the ball')	I am learning to look in response to my name I am learning to understand familiar gestures, words and sounds I am learning to understand gestures I am learning to respond to single key words in a familiar context I am learning to understand simple nouns I am learning to identify an object from its name I am learning to follow simple instructions containing 1 key word	**22 - 36 months** * Identifies action words by pointing to the right picture e.g. 'Who's jumping?' * Understands more complex sentences e.g. 'Put your toys away and then we'll read a book.' * Understands 'who', 'what', 'where' in simple questions (e.g. Who's that/can? What's that? Where is?) * Developing understanding of simple concepts (e.g. big/little) **30 - 50 months** * **Understands use of objects (e.g what do we use to cut things?)** * Shows understanding of prepositions such as 'under', 'on' 'top' 'behind' by carrying out an action or selecting correct picture * Responds to simple instructions e.g. to get or put away an object * Beginning to understand 'why' and 'how' questions

Planning for Learning - Communication & Language: Understanding

Development Matters: Unique Child	Suggested Learning Statements	Looking Ahead
22 - 36 months ✳ Identifies action words by pointing to the right picture e.g. 'Who's jumping?' ✳ Understands more complex sentences e.g. 'Put your toys away and then we'll read a book.' ✳ Understands 'who', 'what', 'where' in simple questions (e.g. Who's that/can? What's that? Where is?) ✳ Developing understanding of simple concepts (e.g. big/little)	I am learning to identify actions in pictures I am learning to follow instructions with 2 parts I am learning to answer "what" "who" "where" questions I am learning to understand simple concepts	**EYFS - ELG** ✳ Children follow instructions involving several ideas or actions ✳ They answer 'how' and 'why' questions about their experiences and in response to stories or events **EYFS - EXCEEDING** ★ After listening to stories children can express views about events or characters in the story and answer questions about why things happened ★ They can carry out instructions which contain several parts in a sequence
30 - 50 months ✳ **Understands use of objects (e.g what do we use to cut things?)** ✳ Shows understanding of prepositions such as 'under', 'on' 'top' 'behind' by carrying out an action or selecting correct picture ✳ Responds to simple instructions e.g. to get or put away an object ✳ Beginning to understand 'why' and 'how' questions	I am learning to follow a simple instruction I am learning to follow instructions that include prepositions	

Planning for Learning - Communication & Language: Understanding

Development Matters: Unique Child	Suggested Learning Statements	Looking Ahead
40 - 60 months ∗ Responds to instructions involving a two-part sequence. Understands humour e.g. nonsense rhymes, jokes ∗ Able to follow a story without pictures or props ∗ Listens and responds to ideas expressed by others in conversation or discussion **EYFS - ELG** ∗ Children follow instructions involving several ideas or actions ∗ They answer 'how' and 'why' questions about their experiences and in response to stories or events	I am learning to follow a 2 part instruction I am learning to ask questions about others' conversation I am learning to follow a story without visual clues I am learning to follow more complex instructions that involve several ideas or actions I am learning to answer "how" and "why" questions about my experiences I am learning to answer "how" and "why" questions in response to stories I am learning to talk about my views and opinions of events or characters in a story I am learning to answer 'why' questions about why things happened in a story I am learning to follow instructions that contain several pieces of information	**EYFS - EXCEEDING** ★ After listening to stories children can express views about events or characters in the story and answer questions about why things happened ★ They can carry out instructions which contain several parts in a sequence **Speaking & Listening Key Stage 1** *(NOTE: these statements are used from Y1 - Y6)* **Pupils should be taught to:** - Listen and respond appropriately to adults and their peers - Ask relevant questions to extend their understanding and build vocabulary and knowledge - Articulate and justify answers, arguments and opinions - Give well-structured descriptions and explanations - Maintain attention and participate actively in collaborative conversations, staying on topic and initiating and responding to comments - Use spoken language to develop understanding through speculating, hypothesising, imagining and exploring ideas - Speak audibly and fluently with an increasing command of Standard English - Participate in discussions, presentations, performances and debates - Gain, maintain and monitor the interest of the listener(s) - Consider and evaluate different viewpoints, attending to and building on the contribution of others - Select and use appropriate registers for effective communication

Planning for Learning - Communication & Language: Speaking

Development Matters: Unique Child	Suggested Learning Statements	Looking Ahead
Birth - 11 months * Communicates needs and feelings a variety of ways including crying, gurgling, babbling and squealing * Makes own sounds in response when talked to by familiar adults * **Lifts arms in anticipation of being picked up** * Practises and gradually develops speech sounds (babbling) to communicate with adults; says sounds like 'baba, nono, gogo' **8 - 20 months** * Uses sounds in play e.g. 'brrrm' for toy car * Uses single words * **Frequently imitates words and sounds** * Enjoys babbling and increasingly experiments with using sounds and words to communicate for a range of purposes (e.g. teddy, more, no, bye-bye) * Uses pointing with eye gaze to make requests and to share an interest * **Creates personal words as they begin to develop language** **16 - 26 months** * Copies familiar expressions e.g 'Oh dear' 'All gone' * Beginning to put two words together (e.g. 'want ball', 'more juice') * Uses different types of everyday words (nouns, verbs and adjectives e.g. 'banana, go, sleep, hot') * Beginning to ask simple questions * Beginning to talk about people and things that are not present	I am learning to communicate my needs and feelings orally I am learning to use sounds to communicate I am learning to make speech sounds I am learning to use sounds to accompany objects in my play I am learning to use single words I am learning to use a combination of sounds and words to communicate I am learning to make my needs and wishes known using non-verbal communication I am learning to say words and phrases that I hear I am learning to put 2 words together in my talk I am learning to use nouns, verbs and adjectives in my talk I am learning to ask a simple question I am learning to talk about people and things that I can not see	**22 - 36 months** * **Uses language as a powerful means of widening contacts, sharing feelings, experiences and thoughts** * Holds a conversation, jumping from topic to topic * Learns new words very rapidly and is able to use them in communicating * **Uses gestures, sometimes with limited talk e.g. reaches toward toy saying 'I have it.'** * Uses a variety of questions (e.g. what, where who) * **Uses simple sentences (e.g. 'Mummy gonna work.')** * Beginning to use word endings (e.g. going, cats) **30 - 50 months** * Beginning to use more complex sentences to link thoughts (e.g. using and, because) * Can retell a simple past event in correct order (e.g. went down slide, hurt finger) * Uses talk to connect ideas, explain what is happening and anticipate what might happen next, recall and relive past experiences * Questions why things happen and gives explanations. Asks e.g. Who, What, When, How? * Uses a range of tenses (e.g. play, playing, will play, played) * Uses intonation, rhythm and phrasing to make the meaning clear to others * **Uses vocabulary focused on objects and people that are of particular importance to them** * Builds up vocabulary that reflects the breadth of their experiences * Uses talk in pretending that objects stand for something else in play, e,g, 'This box is my castle.'

Planning for Learning - Communication & Language: Speaking

Development Matters: Unique Child	Suggested Learning Statements	Looking Ahead
22 - 36 months ✳ **Uses language as a powerful means of widening contacts, sharing feelings, experiences and thoughts** ✳ Holds a conversation, jumping from topic to topic ✳ Learns new words very rapidly and is able to use them in communicating ✳ **Uses gestures, sometimes with limited talk e.g. reaches toward toy saying *'I have it.'*** ✳ Uses a variety of questions *(e.g. what, where, who)* ✳ Uses simple sentences *(e.g. 'Mummy gonna work.')* ✳ Beginning to use word endings *(e.g. going, cats)* **30 - 50 months** ✳ Beginning to use more complex sentences to link thoughts (e.g. using and, because) ✳ Can retell a simple past event in correct order (e.g. went down slide, hurt finger) ✳ Uses talk to connect ideas, explain what is happening and anticipate what might happen next, recall and relive past experiences ✳ Questions why things happen and gives explanations. Asks e.g. Who, What, When, How? ✳ Uses a range of tenses (e.g. play, playing, will play, played) ✳ Uses intonation, rhythm and phrasing to make the meaning clear to others ✳ **Uses vocabulary focused on objects and people that are of particular importance to them** ✳ Builds up vocabulary that reflects the breadth of their experiences ✳ Uses talk in pretending that objects stand for something else in play, e,g, 'This box is my castle.'	I am learning to use new words in my talking I am learning to take turns in a conversation I am learning to ask "what" "who" "where" questions I am learning to talk in simple sentences I am learning to use word endings I am learning to use joining words in my talk I am learning to retell something that happened in the right order I am learning to explain what is happening I am learning to predict what might happen I am learning to talk about an event in the past I am learning to use simple question words I am learning to explain why things happen I am learning to use different tenses in my talk I am learning to use my voice to engage the listener I am learning to use new words appropriately I am learning to talk about who I am pretending to be and what I am pretending to do	**EYFS - ELG** ✳ Children express themselves effectively, showing awareness of listeners' needs ✳ They use past, present and future forms accurately when talking about events that have happened or are to happen in the future ✳ They develop their own narratives and explanations by connecting ideas or events **EYFS - EXCEEDING** ★ Children show some awareness of the listener by making changes to language and non-verbal features ★ They recount experiences and imagine possibilities, often connecting ideas ★ They use a range of vocabulary in imaginative ways to add information , express ideas or to explain or justify actions or events

Planning for Learning - Communication & Language: Speaking

Development Matters: Unique Child	Suggested Learning Statements	Looking Ahead
40 - 60 months * Extends vocabulary especially by grouping and naming, exploring the meaning and sounds of new words * Use language to imagine and recreate roles and experiences in play situations * Links statements and sticks to a main theme or intention * Uses talk to organise, sequence and clarify thinking, ideas, feelings and events * Introduces a storyline or narrative into their play	I am learning to keep to a topic when I talk I am learning to talk clearly about what I am thinking I am learning to talk about my ideas I am learning to talk about my feelings I am learning to tell stories orally I am learning new vocabulary I am learning to talk about events in sequence	**EYFS - EXCEEDING** ★ Children show some awareness of the listener by making changes to language and non-verbal features ★ They account experiences and imagine possibilities, often connecting ideas ★ They use a range of vocabulary in imaginative ways to add information, express ideas or to explain or justify actions or events
EYFS - ELG * Children express themselves effectively, showing awareness of listeners' needs * They use past, present and future forms accurately when talking about events that have happened or are to happen in the future * They develop their own narratives and explanations by connecting ideas or events	I am learning to be fluent and coherent when I talk to others I am learning to adapt my talk in response to how the listener responds I am learning to use the correct tense in my talk I am learning to describe and explain events and my ideas I am learning to connect a series of ideas when talking about my experiences I am leaning to use a wide range of vocabulary in imaginative ways	**Speaking & Listening Key Stage 1** (NOTE: these statements are used from Y1 - Y6) **Pupils should be taught to:** * Listen and respond appropriately to adults and their peers * Ask relevant questions to extend their understanding and build vocabulary and knowledge * Articulate and justify answers, arguments and opinions * Give well-structured descriptions and explanations * Maintain attention and participate actively in collaborative conversations, staying on topic and initiating and responding to comments * Use spoken language to develop understanding through speculating, hypothesising, imaging and exploring ideas * Speak audibly and fluently with an increasing command of Standard English * Participate in discussions, presentation, performances and debates * Gain maintain and monitor the interest of the listener(s) * Consider and evaluate different viewpoints, attending to and building on the contributions of others * Select and use appropriate registers for effective communication

Physical Development

Planning for Learning - Physical Development: Moving & Handling

Development Matters: Unique Child	Suggested Learning Statements	Looking Ahead
Birth - 11 months * Turns head in response to sounds and sights * Gradually develops ability to hold up own head * Makes movements with arms and legs which gradually become more controlled * Rolls over from front to back, from back to front * When lying on tummy becomes able to lift first head and then chest, supporting self with forearms and then straight arms * **Watches and explores hands and feet, e.g. when lying on back lifts legs into vertical position and grasps feet** * Reaches out for, touches and begins to hold objects * Explores objects with mouth, often picking up an object and holding it to the mouth **8 - 20 months** * Sits unsupported on the floor * When sitting, can lean forward to pick up small toys * Pulls to standing, holding on to furniture or person for support * **Crawls, bottom shuffles or rolls continuously to move around** * Walks around furniture lifting one foot and stepping sideways (cruising) and walks with one or high hands held by adult * Takes first few steps independently * Passes toys from one hand to the other * Holds an object in each hand and brings them together in the middle e.g. holds 2 blocks and bangs them together * Picks up small objects between thumb and fingers * **Enjoys the sensory experience of making marks in damp sand, paste or paint** * Holds pen or crayon using whole hand (palmar) grasp and makes random marks with different strokes **16 - 26 months** * Walks upstairs holding hand of adult * Comes downstairs backwards on knees (crawling) * Beginning to balance blocks to build a small tower * **Makes connections between their movements and the marks they make**	I am learning to turn my head in response to things I see and hear I am learning to develop my upper body strength to raise my head I am learning to develop my core stability in order to move my arms and legs I am learning to roll over I am learning to support myself with my arms I am learning to reach out for objects I am learning to hold objects I am learning to mouth objects I am learning to use my core stability to sit unsupported and reach for toys from sitting I am learning to move around my environment independently I am learning to walk by holding onto objects or people I am learning to walk independently I am learning to pass objects from 1 hand to the other I am learning to use 2 hands together when both hands are doing the same thing I am learning to pick up objects between my thumb and fingers I am learning to use a palmer grip I am learning to make random marks with mark making tools I am learning to walk up stairs holding an adult's hand I am learning to come downstairs backwards on my knees I am learning to balance blocks on top of each other	**22 - 36 months** * Runs safely on whole foot * Squats with steadiness to rest or play with object on the ground and rises to feet without using hands * Climbs confidently and is beginning to pull themselves up on nursery play climbing equipment * Can kick a large ball * **Turns pages in a book, sometimes several at once** * Shows control in holding and using jugs to pour, hammers, books and mark-making tools * Beginning to use three fingers (tripod grip) to hold writing tools * Imitates drawing simple shapes such as circles and lines * Walks upstairs or downstairs holding onto a rail two feet to a step * **May be beginning to show preference for dominant hand** **30 - 50 months** * Moves freely and with pleasure and confidence in a range of ways, such as slithering, shuffling, rolling, crawling, walking, running, jumping, skipping, sliding and hopping. * Mounts stairs, steps or climbing equipment using alternative feet * **Walks downstairs, two feet to each step while carrying a small object** * Runs skilfully and negotiates space successfully, adjusting speed or direction to avoid obstacles * Can stand momentarily on one foot when shown * Can catch a large ball * Draws lines and circles using gross motor movements * Uses one-handed tools and equipment e.g. makes snips in paper with child scissors * Holds pencil between thumb and two fingers, no longer using whole-hand grasp * Hold pencil near point between first two fingers and thumb and uses it with good control * Can copy some letters e.g. letters from their name

Planning for Learning - Physical Development: Moving & Handling

Development Matters: Unique Child	Suggested Learning Statements	Looking Ahead
22 - 36 months * Runs safely on whole foot * Squats with steadiness to rest or play with object on the ground and rises to feet without using hands * Climbs confidently and is beginning to pull themselves up on nursery play climbing equipment * Can kick a large ball * **Turns pages in a book, sometimes several at once** * Shows control in holding and using jugs to pour, hammers, books and mark-making tools * Beginning to use three fingers (tripod grip) to hold writing tools * Imitates drawing simple shapes such as circles and lines * Walks upstairs or downstairs holding onto a rail two feet to a step * **May be beginning to show preference for dominant hand** **30 - 50 months** * Moves freely and with pleasure and confidence in a range of ways, such as slithering, shuffling, rolling, crawling, walking, running, jumping, skipping, sliding and hopping. * Mounts stairs, steps or climbing equipment using alternative feet * **Walks downstairs, two feet to each step while carrying a small object** * Runs skilfully and negotiates space successfully, adjusting speed or direction to avoid obstacles * Can stand momentarily on one foot when shown * Can catch a large ball * Draws lines and circles using gross motor movements * Uses one-handed tools and equipment e.g. makes snips in paper with child scissors * Holds pencil between thumb and two fingers, no longer using whole-hand grasp * Hold pencil near point between first two fingers and thumb and uses it with good control * Can copy some letters e.g. letters from their name	I am learning to balance when running I am learning to squat down and rise back up with balance I am learning to climb confidently on and off equipment I am learning to kick a large ball I am learning to control small equipment I am learning to use a tripod grip I am learning to draw simple shapes I am learning to negotiate steps and stairs I am learning to move in a range of ways I am learning to climb using alternate feet I am learning to negotiate space adjusting my speed and/or my direction to avoid obstacles I am learning to balance on one foot I am learning to catch I am learning to draw lines and circles using my whole arm I am learning to use one handed tools I am learning to hold my pencil using a pincer grip I am learning to copy some letter shapes I am learning to control my pencil using a pincer grip	**EYFS - ELG** * Children show good control and co-ordination in large and small movement * They move confidently in a range of ways, safely negotiating space * They handle equipment and tools effectively including pencils for writing **EYFS - EXCEEDING** ★ Children can hop confidently and skip in time to music ★ They hold paper in position and use their preferred hand for writing, using a correct pencil grip ★ They are beginning to be able to write on lines and control letter size

Planning for Learning - Physical Development: Moving & Handling

Development Matters: Unique Child	Suggested Learning Statements	Looking Ahead
40 - 60 months * **Experiments with different ways of moving** * Jumps off an object and lands appropriately * Negotiates space successfully when playing racing and chasing games with other children, adjusting speed or changing direction to avoid obstacles * Travels with confidence and skill around, under, over and through balancing and climbing equipment * Shows increasing control over an object in pushing, patting, throwing, catching or kicking it * Uses simple tools to effect changes to materials * Handles tools, objects, construction and malleable materials safely and with increasing control * **Shows a preference for a dominant hand** * Begins to use anti-clockwise movement and retrace vertical lines * Begins to form recognisable letters * Uses a pencil and holds it effectively to form recognisable letters, most of which are correctly formed **EYFS - ELG** * Children show good control and co-ordination in large and small movement * They move confidently in a range of ways, safely negotiating space * They handle equipment and tools effectively including pencils for writing	I am learning to jump off an object and land appropriately I am learning to travel around, under, over and through equipment I am learning to control small apparatus I am learning to use anti-clockwise movements I am learning to retrace vertical lines I am learning to form recognisable letters when writing independently I am learning to form my letters correctly I am learning to control and manipulate different tools safely I am learning to control and co-ordinate my movements on and off equipment I am learning to handle equipment and tools with dexterity I am learning to hop I am learning to skip in time to music I am learning to use the correct pencil grip I am learning to keep my writing on a line I am learning to form letters of a uniform size	**EYFS - EXCEEDING** ★ Children can hop confidently and skip in time to music ★ They hold paper in position and use their preferred hand for writing, using a correct pencil grip ★ They are beginning to be able to write on lines and control letter size **Physical Education: Key Stage 1** Pupils should be taught to: * Master basic movements including running, jumping, throwing and catching, as well as developing balance, agility and co-ordination, and begin to apply these in a range of activities * Participate in team games, developing simple tactics for attacking and defending * Perform dances using simple movement patterns **Design & Technology: Key Stage 1** Pupils should be taught to: * Design purposeful, functional, appealing products for themselves and other users based on design criteria * Generate, develop, model and communicate their ideas through talking, drawing, templates, mock-ups and, where appropriate, information and communication technology * Select from and use a range of tools & equipment to perform practical tasks such as cutting, shaping, joining & finishing * Select from and use a wide range of materials and components, including construction materials, textiles and ingredients, according to their characteristics * Explore and evaluate a range of existing products * Evaluate their ideas and products against design criteria * Build structures, exploring how they can be made stronger, stiffer and more stable * Explore and use mechanisms, such as levers, sliders, wheels and axles, in their products

Planning for Learning - Physical Development: Health & Self-care

Development Matters: Unique Child	Suggested Learning Statements	Looking Ahead
Birth - 11 months * **Responds to and thrives on warm, sensitive physical contact and care** * **Expresses discomfort, hunger or thirst** * **Anticipates food routines with interest** **8 - 20 months** * **Opens mouth for spoon** * Holds own bottle or cup * Grasps finger food and brings them to mouth * Attempts to use spoon: can guide towards mouth but food often falls off * **Can actively co-operate with nappy changing (lies still, helps hold legs up)** * Starts to communicate urination and bowel movement **16 - 26 months** * **Develops own likes and dislikes in food and drink** * Willing to try new food textures and tastes * Holds cup with both hands and drinks without much spilling * Clearly communicates wet or soiled nappy or pants * **Shows some awareness of bladder and bowel urges** * Shows awareness of what a potty or toilet is used for * Shows a desire to help with dressing/undressing and hygiene routines	I am learning to hold my own bottle or cup I am learning to finger feed myself I am learning to show an awareness of urination and bowel movement I am learning to pick up food on a spoon I am learning to try new foods I am learning to drink from an open cup using 2 hands together I am learning to tell someone when I am wet or soiled I am learning to use the potty/toilet when taken to it I am learning to co-operate with dressing and hygiene routines	**22 - 36 months** * Feeds self competently with spoon * Drinks well without spilling * Clearly communicates their need for potty or toilet * Beginning to recognise danger and seeks support of significant adults for help * Helps with clothing e.g. puts on hat, unzips zipper on jacket, takes off unbuttoned shirt * **Beginning to be independent in self-care, but still often needs adult support** **30 - 50 months** * Can tell adults when hungry or tired or when they want to rest or play * Observes the effect of activity on their bodies * Understands that equipment and tools have to be used safely * Gains more bowel and bladder control and can attend to toileting needs most of the time themselves * Can usually manage washing and drying hands * Dresses with help e.g. puts arms into open-fronted coat or shirt when held up, pulls up own trousers, and pulls up zipper once it is fastened at the bottom

Planning for Learning - Physical Development: Health & Self-care

Development Matters: Unique Child	Suggested Learning Statements	Looking Ahead
22 - 36 months ∗ Feeds self competently with spoon ∗ Drinks well without spilling ∗ Clearly communicates their need for potty or toilet ∗ Beginning to recognise danger and seeks support of significant adults for help ∗ Helps with clothing e.g. puts on hat, unzips zipper on jacket, takes off unbuttoned shirt ∗ **Beginning to be independent in self-care, but still often needs adult support**	I am learning to feed myself with a spoon I am learning to drink from an open cup I am learning to tell someone when I need the toilet I am learning to ask for help when I need it I am learning that some situations are dangerous I am learning to dress myself with help	**EYFS - ELG** ∗ Children know the importance for good health of physical exercise and a healthy diet and talk about ways to keep healthy and safe ∗ They manage their own basic hygiene and personal needs successfully, including dressing and going to the toilet independently **EYFS - EXCEEDING** ★ Children know about and can make healthy choices in relation to healthy eating and exercise ★ They can dress and undress independently, successfully managing fastening buttons or laces
30 - 50 months ∗ Can tell adults when hungry or tired or when they want to rest or play ∗ Observes the effect of activity on their bodies ∗ Understands that equipment and tools have to be used safely ∗ Gains more bowel and bladder control and can attend to toileting needs most of the time themselves ∗ Can usually manage washing and drying hands ∗ Dresses with help e.g. puts arms into open-fronted coat or shirt when held up, pulls up own trousers, and pulls up zipper once it is fastened at the bottom	I am learning to talk to adults about my needs I am learning to talk about how my body feels I am learning to go to the toilet independently I am learning to wash and dry my own hands I am learning to dress myself I am learning to talk about how and why tools must be used safely	

Planning for Learning in Early Years

Planning for Learning - Physical Development: Health & Self-care

Development Matters: Unique Child	Suggested Learning Statements	Looking Ahead
40 - 60 months ✷ **Eats a healthy range of foodstuffs and understands need for variety in food** ✷ **Usually dry and clean during the day** ✷ Shows some understanding that good practices with regard to exercise, eating, sleeping and hygiene can contribute to good health ✷ Shows understanding of the need for safety when tackling new challenges and considers and manages some risks ✷ Shows understanding of how to transport and store equipment safely ✷ Practices some appropriate safety measures without direct supervision **EYFS - ELG** ✷ Children know the importance for good health of physical exercise and a healthy diet and talk about ways to keep healthy and safe ✷ They manage their own basic hygiene and personal needs successfully, including dressing and going to the toilet independently	I am learning how to keep healthy I am learning how to use equipment safely and manage my own risks I am learning how to eat healthily and keep fit I am learning how to keep myself safe I am learning to dress and undress myself independently I am learning to manage my own personal hygiene needs I am learning to make healthy choices I am learning to dress and undress independently I am learning to do fastenings independently	**EYFS - EXCEEDING** ★ Children know about and can make healthy choices in relation to healthy eating and exercise ★ They can dress and undress independently, successfully managing fastening buttons or laces **Physical Education: Key Stage 1** **Pupils should be taught to:** • Master basic movements including running, jumping, throwing and catching, as well as developing balance, agility and co-ordination, and begin to apply these in a range of activities • Participate in team games, developing simple tactics for attacking and defending • Perform dances using simple movement patterns **Design & Technology: Key Stage 1** **Pupils should be taught to:** • Design purposeful, functional, appealing products for themselves and other users based on design criteria • Generate, develop, model and communicate their ideas through talking, drawing, templates, mock-ups and, where appropriate, information and communication technology • Select from and use a range of tools & equipment to perform practical tasks such as cutting, shaping, joining & finishing • Select from and use a wide range of materials and components, including construction materials, textiles and ingredients, according to their characteristics • Explore and evaluate a range of existing products • Evaluate their ideas and products against design criteria • Build structures, exploring how they can be made stronger, stiffer and more stable • Explore and use mechanisms, such as levers, sliders, wheels and axles, in their products

Literacy

Planning for Learning - Literacy: Reading

Development Matters: Unique Child	Suggested Learning Statements	Looking Ahead
Birth - 11 months ✶ **Enjoys looking at books and other printed material with familiar people** **8 - 20 months** ✶ **Handles books and printed material with interest** **16 - 26 months** ✶ Interested in books and rhymes and may have favourites	I am learning to communicate which rhymes and stories I like	**22 - 36 months** ✶ Has some favourite stories, rhymes, songs, poems or jingles ✶ Repeats words or phrases from familiar stories ✶ Fills in the missing word or phrase in a known rhyme, story or game, e.g. Humpty Dumpty sat on a …. **30 - 50 months** ✶ **Enjoys rhyming and rhythmic activities** ✶ Shows awareness of rhyme and alliteration ✶ Recognises rhythm in spoken words ✶ Listens to and joins in with stories and poems, one-to-one and also in small groups ✶ Joins in with repeated refrains and anticipates key events and phrases in rhymes and stories ✶ Beginning to be aware of the way stories are structured ✶ Suggests how the story might end ✶ Listens to stories with increasing attention and recall ✶ Describes main story settings, events and principal characters ✶ **Shows interest in illustrations and print in books and print in the environment** ✶ Recognises familiar words and signs such as own name and advertising logos ✶ **Looks at books independently** ✶ **Handles books carefully** ✶ **Knows information can be relayed in the from of print** ✶ **Holds books the correct way up and turns pages** ✶ Knows that print carries meaning and, in English, is read from left to right and top to bottom

Planning for Learning - Literacy: Reading

Development Matters: Unique Child	Suggested Learning Statements	Looking Ahead
22 - 36 months ✳ Has some favourite stories, rhymes, songs, poems or jingles ✳ Repeats words or phrases from familiar stories ✳ Fills in the missing word or phrase in a known rhyme, story or game e.g. Humpty Dumpty sat on a ….	I am learning to say the missing word or phrase when joining in with familiar rhymes and stories	**EYFS - ELG** ✳ Children read and understand simple sentences ✳ They use phonic knowledge to decode regular words and read them aloud accurately ✳ They also read some common irregular words ✳ They demonstrate understanding when talking with others about what they have read
30 - 50 months ✳ **Enjoys rhyming and rhythmic activities** ✳ Shows awareness of rhyme and alliteration ✳ Recognises rhythm in spoken words ✳ Listens to and joins in with stories and poems, one-to-one and also in small groups ✳ Joins in with repeated refrains and anticipates key events and phrases in rhymes and stories ✳ Beginning to be aware of the way stories are structured ✳ Suggests how the story might end ✳ Listens to stories with increasing attention and recall ✳ Describes main story settings, events and principal characters ✳ **Shows interest in illustrations and print in books and print in the environment** ✳ Recognises familiar words and signs such as own name and advertising logos ✳ **Looks at books independently** ✳ **Handles books carefully** ✳ **Knows information can be relayed in the form of print** ✳ **Holds book the correct way up and turns pages** ✳ Knows that print carries meaning and, in English, is read from left to right and top to bottom	I am learning to listen to stories and poems I am learning to join in with stories and poems I am learning to recognise that some words sound the same I am learning to recognise that some words start with the same sound I am learning to copy a simple rhythm I am learning to keep in time to a beat I am learning to talk about the beginning, middle and end of a story I am learning to make up my own endings to stories I am learning to talk about settings, events and characters I am learning to recognise familiar words and signs I am learning to read left to right and top to bottom	**EYFS - EXCEEDING** ★ Children can read phonically regular words of more than one syllable ★ Children can read irregular high frequency words ★ Children can use phonic, semantic & syntactic knowledge to understand familiar vocabulary ★ Children can describe the main events in the simple stories they have read

Planning for Learning in Early Years

Planning for Learning - Literacy: Reading

Development Matters: Unique Child	Suggested Learning Statements	Looking Ahead
40 - 60 months * Continues a rhyming string * Hears and says the initial sound in words * Can segment the sounds in simple words and blend them together and knows which letters represent some of them * Links sounds to letters, naming and sounding the letters of the alphabet * Begins to read words and simple sentences * Uses vocabulary and forms of speech that are increasingly influenced by their experiences of books * **Enjoys an increasing range of books** * Knows that information can be retrieved from books and computers **EYFS - ELG** * Children read and understand simple sentences * They use phonic knowledge to decode regular words and read them aloud accurately * They also read some common irregular words * They demonstrate understanding when talking with others about what they have read	I am learning to make a set of rhyming words I am learning to hear and say initial sounds in words I am learning to segment sounds in simple words and blend them together I am learning which letter shapes represent sounds I am learning the names and sounds of letters of the alphabet I am learning to link graphemes to phonemes I am learning to read simple words and sentences I am learning to use books and computers to widen my knowledge I am learning to read simple sentences I am learning to use my phonic knowledge to decode regular words I am learning to read regular words accurately I am learning to read some common irregular words I am learning to talk about what I have read I am learning to read phonically regular words of more than one syllable I am learning to read irregular high frequency words I am learning to use different strategies to read and understand unfamiliar vocabulary I am learning to describe the main events in simple stories I have read	**EYFS - EXCEEDING** ★ Children can read phonically regular words of more than one syllable ★ Children can read irregular high frequency words ★ Children can use phonic, semantic & syntactic knowledge to understand familiar vocabulary ★ Children can describe the main events in the simple stories they have read **Key Stage 1: Reading Year 1** **Pupils should be taught to:** • Apply phonic knowledge & skills as the route to decode words • Respond speedily with the correct sound to graphemes (letters or groups of letters) for all 40+ phonemes, including, where applicable, alternative sounds for graphemes • Read accurately by blending sounds in unfamiliar words containing GPCs that have been taught • Read common exception words, noting unusual correspondences between spelling and sound and where these occur in the word • Read words containing taught GPCs and -s, -es, -ing, -ed, -er and -est endings • Read other words of more than one syllable that contain taught GPCs • Read words with contractions e.g. I'm, I'll, we'll and understand that the apostrophe represents the omitted letter(s) • Read aloud accurately books that are consistent with their developing phonic knowledge and that do not require them to use other strategies to work out words • Re-read these books to build up their fluency and confidence

Planning for Learning - Literacy: Writing

Development Matters: Unique Child	Suggested Learning Statements	Learning Outcomes
Birth - 11 months Children's later writing is based on skills and understandings which they develop as babies and toddlers. Before they can write they need to learn to use spoken language to communicate. Later they learn to write down the words they can say. *See roots of writing in Communication and Language*		**22 - 36 months** ✳ Distinguishes between the different marks they make **30 - 50 months** ✳ Sometimes gives meaning to marks as they draw and paint ✳ Ascribes meanings to marks that they see in different places
8 - 20 months & 16 - 26 months Early mark-making is not the same as writing. It is a sensory and physical experience for babies and toddlers, which they do not yet connect to forming symbols which can communicate meaning. *See roots of mark-making and handwriting in Playing and Exploring and Physical Development*	I am learning that I can make marks by moving my body	

Planning for Learning - Literacy: Writing

Development Matters: Unique Child	Suggested Learning Statements	Learning Outcomes
22 - 36 months ✳ Distinguishes between the different marks they make **30 - 50 months** ✳ Sometimes gives meaning to marks as they draw and paint ✳ Ascribes meanings to marks that they see in different places	I am learning to notice the difference between the marks that I make I am learning to comment on the marks that I make I am learning to comment on marks I see in familiar places	**EYFS - ELG** ✳ Children use their phonic knowledge to write words in ways which match their spoken sounds ✳ They also write some irregular common words ✳ They write simple sentences which can be read by themselves and others ✳ Some words are spelt correctly and others are phonetically plausible **EYFS - EXCEEDING** ★ Children can spell phonically regular words of more than one syllable ★ They spell many irregular but high frequency words ★ They use key features of narrative in their own writing

Planning for Learning in Early Years

Planning for Learning - Literacy: Writing

Development Matters: Unique Child	Suggested Learning Statements	Learning Outcomes
40 - 60 months * Gives meaning to marks they make as they draw, write and paint * Begins to break the flow of speech into words * Continues a rhyming string * Hears and says the initial sound in words * Can segment the sounds in simple words and blend them together * Links sounds to letters, naming and sounding the letters of the alphabet * Uses some clearly identifiable letters to communicate meaning, representing some sounds correctly and in sequence * Writes own name and other things such as labels, captions * Attempts to write short sentences in meaningful contexts **EYFS - ELG** * Children use their phonic knowledge to write words in ways which match their spoken sounds * They also write some irregular common words * They write simple sentences which can be read by themselves and others * Some words are spelt correctly and others are phonetically plausible	I am learning to give meanings to marks that I make I am learning to continue a rhyming string I am learning that a sentence has lots of words I am learning to break my sentence into individual words so I can write it down I am learning to write the first sound of each word in my sentence I am learning to write the same number of words on my paper as in my spoken sentence I am learning to write the sounds in simple words I am learning to segment and blend sounds in sequence, in simple words as I write I am learning to write a letter shape in response to its sound and/or name I am learning to write my own name I am learning to write labels, captions & short sentences I am learning to spell phonetically I am learning to spell irregular common words I am learning to read my own writing I am learning to spell phonically regular words of more than one syllable I am learning to include a beginning, middle and end in my writing I am learning to describe the plot and characters in my writing I am learning to use interesting and varied vocabulary in my writing	**EYFS - EXCEEDING** ★ Children can spell phonically regular words of more than one syllable ★ They spell many irregular but high frequency words ★ They use key features of narrative in their own writing **Writing Year 1** **Pupils should be taught to write sentences by:** * Saying out loud what they are going to write about * Composing a sentence orally before writing it * Sequencing sentences to form short narratives * Re-reading what they have written to check that it makes sense * Discuss what they have written with the teacher or other pupils * Read aloud their writing clearly enough to be heard by their peers and teacher **Pupils should be taught to:** * Leave spaces between words * Join words and join sentences using 'and' * Begin to punctuate sentences using a capital letter and a full stop, question mark or exclamation mark * Use a capital letter for names of people, places, the days of the week, and the personal pronoun 'I'

Mathematics

Planning for Learning - Mathematics: Numbers

Development Matters: Unique Child	Suggested Learning Statements	Looking Ahead
Birth - 11 months * Notices changes in number of objects/images or sounds in group of up to 3	I am learning to recognise when an amount changes	**22 - 36 months** * Selects a small number of objects from a group when asked, for example, *'please give me one'*, *'please give me two'* * Recites some number names in sequence * Creates and experiments with symbols and marks representing ideas of number * Begins to make comparisons between quantities * Uses some language of quantities such as *'more'* and *'a lot'* * Knows that a group of things changes in quantity when something is added or taken away
8 - 20 months * **Develops an awareness of number names through their enjoyment of action rhymes and songs that relate to their experience of numbers** * Has some understanding that things exist, even when out of sight	I am learning to recognise that objects still exist when they are out of sight	**30 - 50 months** * Uses some number names and number language spontaneously * Uses some number names accurately in play * Recites numbers in order to 10 * Knows that numbers identify how many objects are in a set * Beginning to represent numbers using fingers, marks on paper or pictures * Sometimes matches numeral and quantity correctly
16 - 26 months * Knows that things exist, even when out of sight * Beginning to organise and categorise objects, e.g. putting all the teddy bears together or teddies and cars in separate piles * Says some counting words randomly	I am learning to put objects together that are similar I am learning to use counting words randomly	* Shows curiosity about numbers by offering comments or asking questions * Compares two groups of objects, saying when they have the same number * **Shows an interest in number problems** * Separates a group of three or four objects in different ways, beginning to recognise that the total is still the same * **Shows an interest in numerals in the environment** * **Shows an interest in representing numbers** * Realises not only objects, but anything can be counted, including steps, claps, jumps

Planning for Learning - Mathematics: Numbers

Development Matters: Unique Child	Suggested Learning Statements	Looking Ahead
22 - 36 months * Selects a small number of objects from a group when asked, for example, *'please give me one'*, *'please give me two'* * Recites some number names in sequence * Creates and experiments with symbols and marks representing ideas of number * Begins to make comparisons between quantities * Uses some language of quantities such as *'more'* and *'a lot'* * Knows that a group of things changes in quantity when something is added or taken away	I am learning to give a required amount of objects I am learning to say some number names in sequence I am learning to compare different quantities I am learning to talk about quantities I am learning that the quantity will change if things are added or taken away I am learning to represent amounts using marks and symbols	**EYFS - ELG** * Children count reliably with numbers from one to 20, place them in order and say which number is one more or one less than a given number * Using quantities and objects, they add and subtract two single-digit numbers and count on or back to find the answer * They solve problems, including doubling, halving and sharing **EYFS - EXCEEDING** ★ Children estimate a number of objects and check quantities by counting up to 20 ★ They solve practical problems that involve combining groups of 2, 5 or 10, or sharing into equal groups
30 - 50 months * Uses some number names and number language spontaneously * Uses some number names accurately in play * Recites numbers in order to 10 * Knows that numbers identify how many objects are in a set * Beginning to represent numbers using fingers, marks on paper or pictures * Sometimes matches numeral and quantity correctly * Shows curiosity about numbers by offering comments or asking questions * Compares two groups of objects, saying when they have the same number * **Shows an interest in number problems** * Separates a group of three or four objects in different ways, beginning to recognise that the total is still the same * **Shows an interest in numerals in the environment** * **Shows an interest in representing numbers** * Realises not only objects, but anything can be counted, including steps, claps, jumps	I am learning to talk about numbers I am learning to rote count I am learning to count a group of objects I am learning to represent numbers I am learning to match numerals with an amount of objects I am learning to identify when 2 sets of objects have the same amount in them I am learning to divide a group of objects in different ways and know that the total is still the same I am learning that when I am counting the last number I say is the total I am learning that numbers identify how many are in a set I am learning to count actions as well as objects	

Planning for Learning - Mathematics: Numbers

Development Matters: Unique Child	Suggested Learning Statements	Looking Ahead
40 - 60 months ✴ **Recognises some numerals of personal significance** ✴ Recognises numerals 1 - 5 ✴ Counts up to three or four objects by saying one number name for each item ✴ Counts actions or objects which cannot be moved ✴ Counts objects to 10, and beginning to count beyond 10 ✴ Counts out up to six objects from a larger group ✴ Selects the correct numeral to represent 1 to 5, then 1 to 10 objects ✴ Counts an irregular arrangement of up to ten objects ✴ Estimates how many objects they can see and checks by counting them ✴ Uses the language of 'more' and 'fewer' to compare two sets of objects ✴ Finds the total number of items in two groups by counting all of them ✴ Says the number that is one more than a given number ✴ Finds one more or one less from a group of up to five objects then ten objects ✴ In practical activities and discussion, beginning to use the vocabulary involved in adding and subtracting ✴ Records, using marks that they can interpret and explain ✴ Begins to identify own mathematical problems based on own interests and fascinations **EYFS - ELG** ✴ Children count reliably with numbers from one to 20, place them in order and say which number is one more or one less than a given number ✴ Using quantities and objects, they add and subtract two single-digit numbers and count on or back to find the answer ✴ They solve problems, including doubling, halving and sharing	I am learning to recognise numerals 1 to 5 I am learning to count a set of objects by saying one number name for each item I am learning to count actions or objects which cannot be moved I am learning to count out objects from a large group I am learning to select the correct numeral to represent the number of objects in a set I am learning to count an irregular arrangement of objects I am learning to estimate I am learning to use the right language to compare two sets of objects I am learning to count two groups together to find the total I am learning to find 1 more I am learning to find 1 less I am learning to use the right mathematical language when adding and taking away I am learning to use marks to record amounts I am learning to put numbers in order I am learning to add two numbers together I am learning to take away one number from another I am learning to count on I am learning to count back I am learning to share equally a set of objects I am learning that doubling is 2 sets of the same number I am learning to split a group in half I am learning to solve mathematical problems I am learning to estimate an amount of objects and check by counting I am learning to count in groups of 2s, 5s,10s I am learning to share amounts into groups of 2s, 5s,10s	**EYFS - EXCEEDING** ★ Children estimate a number of objects and check quantities by counting up to 20 ★ They solve practical problems that involve combining groups of 2, 5 or 10, or sharing into equal groups **Mathematics Year 1** **Number and place value** Pupils should be taught to: • Count to and across 100, forwards and backwards, beginning with 0 or 1, or from any given number • Count read and write numbers to 100 in numerals; count in multiples e.g. twos, fives and tens • Given a number, identify one more and one less • Identify and represent numbers using objects and pictorial representations including the number line, and use the language of: equal to, more than, less than (fewer), most, least • Read and write numbers from 1 to 20 in numerals and words **Addition and subtraction** Pupils should be taught to: • Read, write and interpret mathematical statements involving addition (+), subtraction (-) and equals (=) signs • Represent and use number bonds and related subtraction facts within 20 • Add and subtract one-digit and two digit numbers to 20, including zero • Solve one-step problems that involve addition and subtraction, using concrete objects and pictorial representations, and missing number problems such as 7 = ? - 9

Planning for Learning - Mathematics: Shape, Space & Measure

Development Matters: Unique Child	Suggested Learning Statements	Looking Ahead
Birth - 11 months **Babies' early awareness of shape, space and measure grows from their sensory awareness and opportunities to observe objects and their movements, and to play and explore** *See Characteristics of Effective Learning - Playing and Exploring and Physical Development* **8 - 20 months** ✹ Recognises big things and small things in meaningful contexts ✹ Gets to know and enjoy daily routines, such as getting-up time, mealtimes, nappy time and bedtime **16 - 26 months** ✹ Attempts, sometimes successfully, to fit shapes into spaces on inset boards or jigsaw puzzles ✹ Uses blocks to create their own simple structures and arrangements ✹ Enjoys filling and emptying containers ✹ Associates a sequence of actions with daily routines ✹ **Beginning to understand that things might happen 'now'**	I am learning that objects vary in size I am learning to recognise the key events in daily routines I am learning to match shapes with their outline I am learning to make simple structures and arrangements I am learning to fill and empty I am learning to recognise the sequence of simple daily routines	**22 - 36 months** ✹ Notices simple shapes and patterns in pictures ✹ Beginning to categorise objects according to properties such as shape or size ✹ Begins to use the language of size ✹ Understands some talk about immediate past and future, e.g. 'before', 'later' or 'soon' ✹ Anticipates specific time-based events such as mealtimes or home time **30 - 50 months** ✹ **Shows an interest in shape and space by playing with shapes or making arrangements with objects** ✹ Shows awareness of similarities of shapes in the environment ✹ Uses positional language ✹ **Shows interest in shape by sustained construction activity or by talking about shapes or arrangements** ✹ **Shows interest in shapes in the environment** ✹ Uses shapes appropriately for tasks ✹ Beginning to talk about the shapes of everyday objects, e.g. 'round, 'tall'

Planning for Learning - Mathematics: Shape, Space & Measure

Development Matters: Unique Child	Suggested Learning Statements	Looking Ahead
22 - 36 months ✳ Notices simple shapes and patterns in pictures ✳ Beginning to categorise objects according to properties such as shape or size ✳ Begins to use the language of size ✳ Understands some talk about immediate past and future, e.g. 'before', 'later' or 'soon' ✳ **Anticipates specific time-based events such as mealtimes or home time**	I am learning to notice simple shapes and patterns I am learning to sort objects I am learning to use language of size I am learning what some simple time words mean	**EYFS - ELG** ✳ Children use everyday language to talk about size, weight, capacity, position, distance, time and money to compare quantities and objects and to solve problems ✳ They recognise, create and describe patterns ✳ They explore characteristics of everyday objects and shapes and use mathematical language to describe them **EYFS - EXCEEDING** ✳ Children estimate, measure, weigh and compare and order objects and talk about properties, position and time
30 - 50 months ✳ **Shows an interest in shape and space by playing with shapes or making arrangements with objects** ✳ Shows awareness of similarities of shapes in the environment ✳ Uses positional language ✳ **Shows interest in shape by sustained construction activity or by talking about shapes or arrangements** ✳ **Shows interest in shapes in the environment** ✳ Uses shapes appropriately for tasks ✳ Beginning to talk about the shapes of everyday objects, e.g. 'round and tall'	I am learning to use positional words I am learning to talk about the shapes of everyday objects I am learning to notice shapes in the environment I am learning to use shapes appropriately in my play	

Planning for Learning - Mathematics: Shape, Space & Measure

Development Matters: Unique Child	Suggested Learning Statements	Looking Ahead

40 - 60 months
* Beginning to use mathematical names for 'solid' 3D shapes and 'flat' 2D shapes, and mathematical terms to describe shapes
* Selects a particular named shape
* Can describe their relative position such as 'behind' or 'next to'
* Orders two or three items by length or height
* Orders two items by weight or capacity
* Uses familiar objects and common shapes to create and recreate patterns and build models
* Uses everyday language related to time
* Beginning to use everyday language related to money
* Orders and sequences familiar events
* Measures short periods of time in simple ways
 	
EYFS - ELG
* Children use everyday language to talk about size, weight, capacity, position, distance, time and money to compare quantities and objects and to solve problems
* They recognise, create and describe patterns
* They explore characteristics of everyday objects and shapes and use mathematical language to describe them
	I am learning to use the correct names for 2-D and 3-D shapes
	I am learning to use mathematical words to describe shapes
	I am learning to identify a shape from its name
	I am learning to use prepositions to describe where something is
	I am learning to order objects by length
	I am learning to order objects by height
	I am learning to order objects by weight
	I am learning to order objects by capacity
	I am learning to talk about time using the correct words
	I am learning to talk about money using the correct words
	I am learning to talk about events in the correct sequence
	I am learning to measure short periods of time in simple ways
	I am learning to use shape to create patterns & build models
	I am learning to recognise and talk about different patterns
	I am learning to make a repeating pattern
	
	I am learning to use the correct vocabulary to talk about size/weight/capacity/position/distance/time/money/quantities/objects/solve problems
	I am learning to identify and describe patterns
	I am learning to make up my own patterns
	I am learning to describe objects and shapes using mathematical vocabulary
	I am learning to estimate/measure/weigh/compare/order objects
	I am learning to talk about the properties of shapes and objects using appropriate mathematical vocabulary
		EYFS - EXCEEDING
		* Children estimate, measure, weigh and compare and order objects and talk about properties, position and time
		
		Mathematics Year 1
		Measurement
		Pupils should be taught to:
		• Compare, describe and solve practical problems for:
		   · lengths and heights
		   · mass/weight
		   · capacity and volume
		   · time (quicker, slower, earlier, later)
		• Measure and begin to record the following:
		   · lengths and heights
		   · mass/weight
		   · capacity and volume
		   · time (hours, minutes, seconds)
		• Recognise and know the value of different denominations of coins and notes
		• Sequence events in chronological order using language such as: before/after, next, first, today, yesterday, tomorrow, morning, afternoon and evening
		• Recognise and use language relating to dates, including days of the week, months and years
		• Tell the time to the hour and half past the hour and draw the hands on a clock to show these times
		
		Properties of shapes
		Pupils should be taught to:
		• Recognise and name common 2-D and 3-D shapes, including:
		   · 2-D shapes (e.g. rectangles (including squares), circles and triangles)
		   · 3-D shapes (e.g. cuboids (including cubes), pyramids and spheres).

Understanding the World

Planning for Learning - Understanding the World: People & Communities

Development Matters: Unique Child	Suggested Learning Statements	Looking Ahead
Birth - 11 months & 8 - 20 months **The beginnings of understanding of People and Communities lie in early attachment and other relationships.** *See Personal, Social and Emotional Development and Communication and Language.* **16 - 26 months** * **Is curious about people and shows interest in stories about themselves and their family** * **Enjoys pictures and stories about themselves, their families and other people**		**22 - 36 months** * **Has a sense of own immediate family and relations** * In pretend play, imitates everyday actions and events from own family and cultural background, e.g. making and drinking tea * Beginning to have their own friends * Learns that they have similarities and differences that connect them to, and distinguish them from, others **30 - 50 months** * Shows interest in the lives of people who are familiar to them * Remembers and talks about significant events in their own experience * Recognises and describes special times or events for family or friends * **Shows interest in different occupations and ways of life** * Knows some of the things that make them unique, and can talk about some of the similarities and differences in relation to friends or family

Planning for Learning - Understanding the World: People & Communities

Development Matters: Unique Child	Suggested Learning Statements	Looking Ahead
22 - 36 months * **Has a sense of own immediate family and relations** * In pretend play, imitates everyday actions and events from own family and cultural background, e.g. making and drinking tea * Beginning to have their own friends * Learns that they have similarities and differences that connect them to, and distinguish them from, others	I am learning to make relationships with other children I am learning to notice that I am the same as some people and different from some people I am learning to act out events from my life at home	**EYFS - ELG** * Children talk about past and present events in their own lives and in the lives of family members * They know that other children don't always enjoy the same things, and are sensitive to this * They know about similarities and differences between themselves and others, and among families, communities and traditions **EYFS - EXCEEDING** * Children know the difference between past and present events in their own lives and some reasons why people's lives were different in the past
30 - 50 months * Shows interest in the lives of people who are familiar to them * Remembers and talks about significant events in their own experience * Recognises and describes special times or events for family or friends * **Shows interest in different occupations and ways of life** * Knows some of the things that make them unique, and can talk about some of the similarities and differences in relation to friends or family	I am learning to talk about people that are important in my life I am learning to talk about important things that have happened to me I am learning to talk about special events in my life I am learning to ask questions about other people's experiences I am learning to talk about how I am the same and different from others	* They know that other children have different likes and dislikes and that they may be good at different things * They understand that different people have different beliefs, attitudes, customs and traditions and why it is important to treat them with respect

Planning for Learning - Understanding the World: People & Communities

Development Matters: Unique Child	Suggested Learning Statements	Looking Ahead
40 - 60 months * Enjoys joining in with family customs and routines **EYFS - ELG** * Children talk about past and present events in their own lives and in the lives of family members * They know that other children don't always enjoy the same things, and are sensitive to this * They know about similarities and differences between themselves and others, and among families, communities and traditions	I am learning to talk about past and present events that happened in my own life I am learning to talk about past and present events that happened in the lives of my family I am learning that other people have different likes and dislikes I am leaning to identify and talk about how I am the same and different from others I am learning to identify and talk about how my family sometimes does things the same as other families and sometimes does things differently I am learning how people celebrate traditions differently I am learning to talk about how people lived in the past I am learning to talk about the differences between how we live now and how it was in the past I am learning to talk about other people's likes, dislikes and strengths I am learning to talk about other people's customs and traditions and explain why they are important to them	**EYFS - EXCEEDING** * Children know the difference between past and present events in their own lives and some reasons why people's lives were different in the past * They know that other children have different likes and dislikes and that they may be good at different things * They understand that different people have different beliefs, attitudes, customs and traditions and why it is important to treat them with respect **History Key Stage 1** * Pupils should develop an awareness of the past, using common words and phrases relating to the passing of time * They should know where the people and events they study fit within a chronological framework and identify similarities and differences between ways of life in different periods * They should use a wide vocabulary of everyday historical terms * They should ask and answer questions, choosing and using parts of stories and other sources to show that they know and understand key features of events * They should understand some of the ways in which we find out about the past and identify different ways in which it is represented **Pupils should be taught about:** * Changes within living memory * Events beyond living memory that are significant nationally or globally * The lives of significant individuals in the past who have contributed to national and international achievements * Significant historical events, people and places in their own locality

Planning for Learning - Understanding the World: The World

Development Matters: Unique Child	Suggested Learning Statements	Looking Ahead
Birth - 11 months * Moves eyes, then head, to follow moving objects * Reacts with abrupt change when a face or object suddenly disappears from view * Looks around a room with interest; visually scans environment for novel, interesting objects and events * **Smiles with pleasure at recognisable playthings** * Repeats actions that have an effect e.g. kicking or hitting a mobile or shaking a rattle *See also Characteristics of Effective Learning - Playing & Exploring and Physical Development*	I am learning to track moving objects I am learning to notice when objects disappear I am learning to scan my environment visually I am learning to recognise cause and effect	**22 - 36 months** * **Enjoys playing with small-world models such as a farm, a garage, or a train track** * Notices detailed features of objects in their environment **30 - 50 months** * Comments and asks questions about aspects of their familiar world such as the place where they live or the natural world * Can talk about some of the things they have observed such as plants, animals, natural and found objects * Talks about why things happen and how things work * Developing an understanding of growth, decay and changes over time * Shows care and concern for living things and the environment
8 - 20 months * Closely observes what animals, people and vehicles do * Watches toy being hidden and tries to find it * Looks for dropped objects * Becomes absorbed in combining objects, e.g. banging two objects or placing objects into containers * Knows things are used in different ways, e.g. a ball for rolling or throwing, a toy car for pushing	I am learning to notice and watch what is going on around me I am learning to find an object when it is hidden in front of me I am learning to look for objects when they have been dropped I am learning to use 2 objects together I am learning to use objects in more than 1 way	
16 - 26 months * Explores objects by linking together different approaches: shaking, hitting, looking, feeling, tasting, mouthing, pulling, turning and poking * Remembers where objects belong * Matches parts of objects that fit together, e.g. puts lid on teapot	I am learning to explore objects using my senses of taste, feel and sight I am learning where objects belong I am learning to match parts of objects that fit together	

Planning for Learning - Understanding the World: The World

Development Matters: Unique Child	Suggested Learning Statements	Looking Ahead
22 - 36 months * **Enjoys playing with small-world models such as a farm, a garage, or a train track** * Notices detailed features of objects in their environment	I am learning to notice and talk about some of the things in my immediate environment	**EYFS - ELG** * Children know about similarities and differences in relation to places, objects, materials and living things * They talk about the features of their own immediate environment and how environments might vary from one another * They make observations of animals and plants and explain why some things occur, and talk about changes
30 - 50 months * Comments and asks questions about aspects of their familiar world such as the place where they live or the natural world * Can talk about some of the things they have observed such as plants, animals, natural and found objects * Talks about why things happen and how things work * Developing an understanding of growth, decay and changes over time * Shows care and concern for living things and the environment	I am learning to ask questions and talk about the world around me I am learning to look carefully at the world around me I am learning to talk about the things I have noticed in the world around me I am learning to talk about why things happen I am learning to talk about how things work I am learning how to look after the world around me I am learning to recognise when and how things change	**EYFS - EXCEEDING** * Children know that the environment and living things are influenced by human activity * They can describe some actions which people in their own community do that help to maintain the area they live in * They know the properties of some materials and can suggest some of the purposes they are used for * They are familiar with basic scientific concepts such as floating, sinking and experimentation

Planning for Learning in Early Years

Planning for Learning - Understanding the World: The World

Development Matters: Unique Child	Suggested Learning Statements	Looking Ahead
40 - 60 months ★ Looks closely at similarities, differences, patterns and change **EYFS - ELG** ★ Children know about similarities and differences in relation to places, objects, materials and living things ★ They talk about the features of their own immediate environment and how environments might vary from one another ★ They make observations of animals and plants and explain why some things occur, and talk about changes	I am learning how things grow I am learning about simple life cycles I am learning to notice and talk about how some things are the same I am learn to notice and talk about how some things are different I am learning to notice and talk about patterns I am learning to notice and talk about changes that take place over time I am learning to notice and talk about similarities and differences between places/objects/materials/plants & animals I am learning to describe places that I am familiar with I am learning to notice and talk about how places are the same and different I am learning to describe the features of plants and animals I am learning to answer 'why' and 'how' questions about animals and plants I am learning to notice and talk about the changes that happen to animals and plants I am learning to talk about how people can protect and destroy the environment and living things I am learning to find out how people protect and look after their local area I am learning to describe the properties of different materials I am learning to make sensible suggestions about what different materials might be used for I am learning to carry out simple fair tests and draw simple conclusions	**EYFS - EXCEEDING** ★ Children know that the environment and living things are influenced by human activity ★ They can describe some actions which people in their own community do that help to maintain the area they live in ★ They know the properties of some materials and can suggest some of the purposes they are used for ★ They are familiar with basic scientific concepts such as floating, sinking and experimentation **Science Year 1** *Plants* Pupils should be taught to: • Identify and name a variety of common plants, including garden plants, wild plants and trees and those classified as deciduous and evergreen • Identify and describe the basic structure of a variety of common flowering plants, including roots, stem/trunk, leaves and flowers *Animals, including humans* Pupils should be taught to: • Identify and name a variety of common animals that are birds, fish, amphibians, reptiles, mammals and invertebrates • Identify and name a variety of common animals that are carnivores, herbivores and omnivores • Describe and compare the structure of a variety of common animals (birds, fish, amphibians, reptiles, mammals and invertebrates, and including pets) • Basic parts of the human body and say which part of the body is associated with each sense **Geography Year 1** ★ Pupils should develop knowledge about the world, the United Kingdom and their locality ★ They should understand basic subject-specific vocabulary relating to human and physical geography and begin to use geographical skills, including first-hand observation, to enhance their locational awareness

Planning for Learning - Understanding the World: Technology

Development Matters: Unique Child	Suggested Learning Statements	Looking Ahead
Birth - 11 months & 8 - 20 months **The beginnings of understanding technology lie in babies exploring and making sense of objets and how they behave** *See Characteristics of Effective Learning - Playing & Exploring and Creating & Thinking Critically* **16 - 26 months** * Anticipates repeated sounds, sights and actions e.g. when an adult demonstrates an action toy several times * Shows interest in toys with buttons, flaps and simple mechanisms and beginning to learn to operate them	I am learning to notice repeated sounds, sights and actions of objects I am learning to operate toys with simple mechanisms	**22 - 36 months** * Seeks to acquire basic skills in turning on and operating some ICT equipment * Operates mechanical toys e.g. turns the knob on a wind-up toy or pulls back on a friction car **30 - 50 months** * Knows how to operate simple equipment, e.g. turns on CD player and uses remote control * **Shows an interest in technological toys with knobs or pulleys, or real objects such as cameras or mobile phones** * Shows skill in making toys work by pressing parts or lifting flaps to achieve effects such as sound, movements or new images * Knows that information can be retrieved from computers

Planning for Learning - Understanding the World: Technology

Development Matters: Unique Child	Suggested Learning Statements	Looking Ahead
22 - 36 months ✳ Seeks to acquire basic skills in turning on and operating some ICT equipment ✳ Operates mechanical toys e.g. turns the knob on a wind-up toy or pulls back on a friction car	I am learning to turn equipment on and off I am learning to operate simple toys	**EYFS - ELG** ✳ Children recognise that a range of technology is used in places such as homes and schools ✳ They select and use technology for particular purposes
30 - 50 months ✳ Knows how to operate simple equipment, e.g. turns on CD player and uses remote control ✳ **Shows an interest in technological toys with knobs or pulleys, or real objects such as cameras or mobile phones** ✳ Shows skill in making toys work by pressing parts or lifting flaps to achieve effects such as sound, movements or new images ✳ Knows that information can be retrieved from computers	I am learning to operate a range of simple technology I am learning that different technology is suitable for different purposes I am learning to operate toys to achieve a desired effect	**EYFS - EXCEEDING** ★ Children find out about and use a range of everyday technology ★ They select appropriate applications that support an identified need - for example in deciding how best to make a record of a special event in their lives, such as a journey on a steam train

Planning for Learning - Understanding the World: Technology

Development Matters: Unique Child	Suggested Learning Statements	Looking Ahead
40 - 60 months * Completes a simple program on a computer * Uses ICT hardware to interact with age-appropriate computer software **EYFS - ELG** * Children recognise that a range of technology is used in places such as homes and schools * They select and use technology for particular purposes	I am learning to use a simple computer program I am learning to choose the appropriate technology for a task I am learning to select an appropriate application for a task when using a range of technology	**EYFS - EXCEEDING** ★ Children find out about and use a range of everyday technology ★ They select appropriate applications that support an identified need - for example in deciding how best to make a record of a special event in their lives, such as a journey on a steam train **Computing Key Stage 1** **Pupils should be taught to:** • Understand what algorithm are; how they are implemented as programs on digital devices; and that programs execute by following precise and unambiguous instructions • Create and debug simple programs • Use logical reasoning to predict the behaviour of simple programs • Use technology purposefully to create, organise, store, manipulate and retrieve digital content • Use technology safely and respectfully, keeping personal information private; know where to go for help and support when they have concerns about material on the internet • Recognise common uses of information technology beyond school

Expressive Arts & Design

Planning for Learning - Expressive Arts & Design: Exploring & Using Media & Materials

Development Matters: Unique Child	Suggested Learning Statements	Looking Ahead
Birth - 11 months **Babies explore media and materials as part of their exploration of the world around them.** *See Characteristics of Effective Learning - Playing & Exploring, Physical Development, Understanding the World - The World*		**22 - 36 months** * Joins in singing favourite songs * Creates sounds by banging, shaking, tapping or blowing * **Shows an interest in the way musical instruments sound** * Experiments with blocks, colours and marks
8 - 20 months & 16 - 26 months * Explores and experiments with a range of media through sensory exploration, and using whole body * Move their whole bodies to sounds they enjoy, such as music or a regular beat * Imitates and improvises actions they have observed e.g. clapping or waving * Begins to move to music, listen to or join in rhymes or songs * **Notices and is interested in the effects of making movements which leave marks**	I am learning to use my senses to explore media I am learning to move my body in response to sounds I am learning to copy the actions that I have seen I am learning to use my body to join in with songs and rhymes	**30 - 50 months** * **Enjoys joining in with dancing and ring games** * Sings a few familiar songs * Beginning to move rhythmically * Imitates movement in response to music * Taps out simple repeated rhythms * Explores and learns how sounds can be changed * Explores colour and how colours can be changed * Understands that they can use lines to enclose a space, and then begin to use these shapes to represent objects * Beginning to be interested in and describe the texture of things * **Uses various construction materials** * Beginning to construct, stacking blocks vertically and horizontally, making enclosures and creating spaces * Joins construction pieces together to build and balance * Realises tools can be used for a purpose

Planning for Learning - Expressive Arts & Design: Exploring & Using Media & Materials

Development Matters: Unique Child	Suggested Learning Statements	Looking Ahead
22 - 36 months ＊ Joins in singing favourite songs ＊ Creates sounds by banging, shaking, tapping or blowing ＊ **Shows an interest in the way musical instruments sound** ＊ Experiments with blocks, colours and marks	I am learning to create sounds I am learn to experiment with different materials and media I am learning to sing songs	**EYFS - ELG** ＊ Children sing songs, make music and dance and experiment with ways of changing them ＊ They safely use and explore a variety of materials, tools and techniques, experimenting with colour, design, texture, form and function
30 - 50 months ＊ **Enjoys joining in with dancing and ring games** ＊ Sings a few familiar songs ＊ Beginning to move rhythmically ＊ Imitates movement in response to music ＊ Taps out simple repeated rhythms ＊ Explores and learns how sounds can be changed ＊ Explores colour and how colours can be changed ＊ Understands that they can use lines to enclose a space, and then begin to use these shapes to represent objects ＊ Beginning to be interested in and describe the texture of things ＊ **Uses various construction materials** ＊ Beginning to construct, stacking blocks vertically and horizontally, making enclosures and creating spaces ＊ Joins construction pieces together to build and balance ＊ Realises tools can be used for a purpose	I am learning to copy movements in response to music I am learning to keep in time to a beat when moving I am learning to tap out a rhythm I have heard I am learning to experiment with sounds to see how they can be changed I am learning to experiment with colours to see how they can be changed I am learning to use lines to create shapes and objects I am learning to talk about how different things feel I am learning to stack, balance and join to build structures I am learning to use tools appropriately	**EYFS - EXCEEDING** ★ Children develop their own ideas through selecting and using materials and working on processes that interest them ★ Through their explorations they find out and make decisions about how media and materials can be combined and changed

Planning for Learning in Early Years

Planning for Learning - Expressive Arts & Design: Exploring & Using Media & Materials

Development Matters: Unique Child	Suggested Learning Statements	Looking Ahead
40 - 60 months * **Begins to build a repertoire of songs and dances** * Explores the different sounds of instruments * Explores what happens when they mix colours * Experiments to create different textures * Understands that different media can be combined to create new effects * Manipulates materials to achieve a planned effect * Constructs with a purpose in mind, using a variety of resources * Uses simple tools and techniques competently and appropriately * Selects appropriate resources and adapts work where necessary * Selects tools and techniques needed to shape, assemble and join materials they are using **EYFS - ELG** * Children sing songs, make music and dance and experiment with ways of changing them * They safely use and explore a variety of materials, tools and techniques, experimenting with colour, design, texture, form and function	I am learning to make different sounds using instruments I am learning to experiment with colour and texture I am learning to mix colours I am learning to select the right tools and techniques to complete a task I am learning that different media creates different effects I am learning to plan what I want to make before I make it I am learning to choose the correct tools for the job I am learning to choose the correct resources for the job I am learning to review my work and change it if I need to I am learning to create and adapt my own songs I am learning to create and adapt my own music I am learning to create and adapt my own dances I am learning to use different materials in different ways I am learning to use different tools, safely, in different ways I am learning to use different techniques in different ways I am learning to extend and develop my ideas I am learning to combine and change different media and materials	**EYFS - EXCEEDING** ★ Children develop their own ideas through selecting and using materials and working on processes that interest them ★ Through their explorations they find out and make decisions about how media and materials can be combined and changed **Design & Technology Key Stage 1** Pupils should be taught to: * Design purposeful, functional, appealing products for themselves and other users based on design criteria * Generate, develop, model and communicate their ideas through talking, drawing, templates, mock-ups and, where appropriate, information and communication technology * Select from and use a range of tools & equipment to perform practical tasks such as cutting, shaping, joining & finishing * Select from and use a wide range of materials and components, including construction materials, textiles and ingredients, according to their characteristics * Explore and evaluate a range of existing products * Evaluate their ideas and products against design criteria * Build structures, exploring how they can be made stronger, stiffer and more stable * Explore and use mechanisms, such as levers, sliders, wheels and axles, in their products **Music Key Stage 1** Pupils should be taught to: * Use their voices expressively and creatively by singing songs and speaking chants and rhymes * Play tuned and untuned instruments musically * Listen with concentration and understanding to a range of high-quality live and recorded music * Experiment with, create, select and combine sounds using the inter-related dimensions of music

Planning for Learning - Expressive Arts & Design: Being Imaginative

Development Matters: Unique Child	Suggested Learning Statements	Looking Ahead
Birth - 11 months & 8 - 20 months Babies and toddlers need to explore the world and develop a range of ways to communicate before they can express their own ideas through arts and design. *See Characteristics of Effective Learning; Communication & Language; Physical Development; Personal, Social & Emotional Development* **16 - 26 months** ✶ **Expresses self through physical action and sound** ✶ Pretends that one object represents another, especially when objects have characteristics in common	I am learning to pretend that one thing is something else	**22 - 36 months** ✶ Beginning to use representation to communicate e.g. drawing a line and saying 'That's me.' ✶ Beginning to make-believe by pretending **30 - 50 months** ✶ **Developing preferences for forms of expression** ✶ Uses movement to express feelings ✶ Creates movement in response to music ✶ **Sings to self and makes up simple songs** ✶ **Makes up rhythms** ✶ **Notices what adults do, imitating what is observed and then doing it spontaneously when the adult is not there** ✶ Engages in imaginative role-play based on own first-hand experiences ✶ Builds stories around toys e.g. farm animals needing rescue from an armchair 'cliff' ✶ Uses available resources to create props to support role play ✶ Captures experiences and responses with a range of media such as music, dance and paint and other materials or words

Planning for Learning in Early Years

Planning for Learning - Expressive Arts & Design: Being Imaginative

Development Matters: Unique Child	Suggested Learning Statements	Looking Ahead
22 - 36 months ✳ Beginning to use representation to communicate e.g. drawing a line and saying 'That's me.' ✳ Beginning to make-believe by pretending	I am learning to play imaginatively by pretending I am learning to talk in simple terms about the 2D or 3D representations that I make	**EYFS - ELG** ✳ Children use what they have learnt about media and materials in original ways, thinking about uses and purposes ✳ They represent their own ideas, thoughts and feelings through design and technology, art, music, dance, role play and stories
30 - 50 months ✳ **Developing preferences for forms of expression** ✳ Uses movement to express feelings ✳ Creates movement in response to music ✳ **Sings to self and makes up simple songs** ✳ **Makes up rhythms** ✳ **Notices what adults do, imitating what is observed and then doing it spontaneously when the adult is not there** ✳ Engages in imaginative role-play based on own first-hand experiences ✳ Builds stories around toys e.g. farm animals needing rescue from an armchair 'cliff' ✳ Uses available resources to create props to support role play ✳ **Captures experiences and responses with a range of media such as music, dance and paint and other materials or words**	I am learning to move in response to music I am learning to pretend to be someone else I am learning to tell my own story I am learning to play imaginatively I am learning to create props for my role play	**EYFS - EXCEEDING** ★ Children talk about the ideas and processes which have led them to make music, designs, images or products ★ They can talk about features of their own and others work, recognising the differences between them and the strengths of others

Planning for Learning in Early Years

Planning for Learning - Expressive Arts & Design: Being Imaginative

Development Matters: Unique Child	Suggested Learning Statements	Looking Ahead
40 - 60 months * Creates simple representations of events, people and objects * Initiates new combinations of movement and gesture in order to express and respond to feelings, ideas and experiences * Chooses particular colours to use for a purpose * Introduces a storyline or narrative into their play * Plays alongside other children who are engaged in the same theme * Plays co-operatively as part of a group to develop and act out a narrative **EYFS - ELG** * Children use what they have learnt about media and materials in original ways, thinking about uses and purposes * They represent their own ideas, thoughts and feelings through design and technology, art, music, dance, role play and stories	I am learning to create simple representations of events, people and objects I am learning to move in different ways to show how I am feeling I am learning to move in different ways to show my ideas I am learning to move in different ways to show my experiences I am learning to choose which colours to use for a purpose I am learning to play alongside others I am learning to play cooperatively with others to act out a story I am learning to create a storyline in my play I am learning to choose different ways to represent my ideas, thoughts and feelings I am learning to use media and materials in original ways I am learning to talk about the ideas and processes that I have used I am learning to talk about the features of my own and others' work I am learning to talk about the differences between my own work and others' work I am learning to describe what I think is good about other people's work and why	**EYFS - EXCEEDING** ★ Children talk about the ideas and processes which have led them to make music, designs, images or products ★ They can talk about features of their own and others work, recognising the differences between them and the strengths of others **Art & Design 1** Pupils should be taught: • To use a range of materials creatively to design and make products • To use drawing, painting and sculpture to develop and share their ideas, experiences and imagination • To develop a wide range of art and design techniques in using colour, pattern, texture, line, shape, form and space • About the work of a range of artists, craft makers and designers, describing the differences and similarities between different practices and disciplines, and making links to their own work